Foreword by the Author

'Politicians cannot be trusted to tell the truth. This is the remit of comedians and poets, nowadays.' I remember the quote. I can't tell you whose words these are.

My job, in creating this volume, has been to make my version of the truth easily accessible and not esoteric. I do hope these works will make you stop, sit up, contemplate and cry, chuckle or even laugh out loud. If I achieve this then all the hard work has been worth it and I can rest assured that I am doing my little bit in this life.

If you are a teacher, invite me to work at your school – you will never regret it. If you would like me to perform stand-up poetry to all ages at any venue for any purpose, please contact me. Together we can make the world a better place with the help of a word or two.

David J. Mason

Enquiries@InspireToWrite.co.uk
www.InspireToWrite.co.uk

GW00746055

Publishing Information

"Tears and Laughter" © David J. Mason 2015
All rights reserved
Publisher: North Street Publishing
Publishing address: North Street Publishing
14 Ribblesdale Avenue Congleton Cheshire CW12 2BS
Telephone: 01260 291898   www.InspireToWrite.co.uk
Email: Enquiries@InspireToWrite.co.uk

ISBN 978-0-9569287-7-1

Printed by Orbital Print Services Ltd

Staplehurst Road, Sittingbourne, Kent ME10 2NH

www.orbitalprint.co.uk

Tears
And
Laughter

Table of Contents

Shorthand

Mrs Jones
Take a letter
No, twenty-six of them.
Now jumble them about
And what have you got?
A sentence, Mr Smith, a sentence!
Make some more sentences
Add them together
Mix them about a bit
Now what have you got?
I don't know Mr Smith,
The sentences, they don't make sense.
But the whole, Mrs Jones, the whole?
Ah, Mr Smith, I see!
The naughty games you play with me
Yes, 'tis poetry, 'tis poetry.

Translation

Only the words
Can take me
Shake me
Make me
Sit up in order
To ponder
The wonder
Of a world
Where words
Are frankly absurd
Blunted tools
Obeying rules
Too tight
To let in light
That just might
Give the right
Notion
Of some emotion.

Poetry Flow

In the corridors of the halls
Of those of future fame
The words never spoken
Were about to be said,
As lava from a volcano
Under pressure explodes
So a seismic shift
And the poetry flows.

Far out from the shores
Deep hope is at hand
And the ocean enraged
By the threat from the land
Bruised and swollen
And spitting his fear
He's gorging the sand
And raining down tears.
His booming voice sounding
The words out of reach
And when the storm calms
They will litter the beach

You can float with the tide
As the poetry flows
Or say you can't swim
And sink as a stone.

Across the great plains
The river is creeping
Fingers feeling for fissures reaching
Defences in the strata breaching
So underground the poetry flows
To caverns hidden 'neath pot holes.
Listen you will hear them talking
Springs the water pure and sparkling
Perfect for the master's drinking
The message begging for the bottling.

A key in the lock
The open road.
Which way to follow
How crack the code?
Should I dance in the streets
Let the poetry flow,
Or block up my ears, declare
Poetry? No.

Hole in the Heart

There's a hole in our heart
And we know it needs filling
With the spirit of life
And the spirit is willing.

There's a whole in our hearts
It's overflowing
With the spirit of life
And the spirit is growing.

Rich and poor

The rich man keeps on
Buying things
Till he is sick to death
Of them

The poor man is very sick
And he will die
Unless someone buys him
Something

I'm dying to buy something
Am I sick
Or poor or
Rich?

Foolish

I have seen it
It is for sale
Everyone has it
It is my turn now.

It is a must-have
I must have it
Now I want it
I want it now.

You have told me
I need it
I hear you
I believe in you.

It will make me happy
If I take it
It will fill the hole of
Aching emptiness inside me...

...It is still with me
I have finished with it
I do not cherish it
I have forgotten it.

I have seen another
It is for sale
Everyone has this other
It is my turn now.

Wise

I have seen it
It is a light
It has shone
Inside my heart.

I cannot deny it
I must follow it
Now I want to
I want to now.

You have told me
I need it
I hear you
I believe you.

I will feel peace
If I follow it
It will fill my life
And make me whole.

It is still with me
It has just begun
It stays with me, everyday
I listen to the spirit.

I do not need another
I have enough
I have found
The light of my life.

Thanks, I'm happy

Thank-you is a thing of the past
Instead you must look
To the next on the list
This is the pointless
Pursuit of
Happiness.

Manners

God gave the sunlight
God gave the water
God is the chef
God is the waiter
God made the plants
God made the creatures
God gave the places
God set the tables

The human race sits down to eat
They say there's not enough.
The humans make a mess of things
- The angels won't clear up.

Jigsaw Pieces

Life is made of jigsaw
Pieces
And everyone's is different from everyone
Else's
The picture we shape should be perfect
Complete
Like everyone else's tidy and
Neat
But mine has holes where pieces are
Missing
And some of those pieces just don't want to
Fit in
Yes life is made of jigsaw
Pieces
Odd and misshapen like everyone
Else's.

One Thought at a Time

There's only the room
For one thought in my head
Another can't sleep
With the other in bed.

There's only the room
For one thought in my head
Another won't scan
Until this one is read.

There's only the room
For one thought in my head
Another can't say
Until this one is said.

There's only the room
For one thought in my head
Another can't live
Until this one is dead.

A Moment

A tiny bird
A beautiful bird
Called Moment
Flew to my hand
She was nervous
So was I
I did not move
In case she left me
She was beautiful
I saw
I listened
I dared to stroke her wing
As she settled in my palm
And through my fingers
I felt her soft heart beating.
Hang on a moment
I whispered to her
Her song was all soothing
Sent shivers through me
I shall stay as long
As you let me
And when I am gone
You must never forget me
The future you fashion
Is nothing to me
I am your moment
Come, let us be.

So soft

So soft
The gentle rain
Falls upon the
Fields far and near
So soft
The passing breath
Of the breeze
Through the woodlands
So soft
The spill of sea
Salt and foam
On the
Shoreline
So soft
The brush of honey bee
With the flower
Dancing cheek to cheek
So soft
The mysterious voice
Of Nature
Calling us
So hard for us to listen
So hard for us to learn
So softly we must turn
Our waiting world around.

Wait a While

Wait a while
Don't move
Silent and still
Just you
Waiting a while
Nothing happened
Nothing will
Just now
Wait a while
Whatever you do
Or rather whatever you don't
It's worth that while.

In the Silence

In the silence
You will want
To fill the emptiness.
And you will feel
Afraid and helpless.
You will open your hands
To touch nothing
Your eyes to see everything
And you will whisper
Hello
But no one will answer
You
Until you learn to talk
From the very bottom
Of your heart.

A Rest

Looking out over the sun
I would rise above it, weightless,
Dropping anchor on this turning globe.
Motionless at high noon,
I would accommodate nothing
Lose all sense
Of being, beat and pulse
Of blood and flesh.
I am a museum piece
Stricken by siesta
Tired of turning out
Day after day
Turning into an angel
Or a ghost
I'll let you know
When I begin again.

When I grow down

When I grow down
I want to be
More of a seedling
And less of a tree
Or at least
Find the seedling
Inside of me.

First Day

Her eyes are brimming with tears
She struggles with a smile
To hide the deepest fears
She surely feels
His hot hand clings to hers
His little boy's face says
I don't know, I'm not certain,
Cross his heart, he draws a curtain.
He is a brave boy
A big boy does not cry
He checks for the smile in his mother's eye
His mother will not cry
One last good-bye.
He drags the cooling hand
Lifting makes a limp wave
In the harbour he sees her
Flag hands fluttering
I love you darling.

A wind of change blows him
A turning tide takes him
Sailing into the classroom
All at sea, whilst she
Head bowed towards the empty buggy
Pushes on through crowds of mums
She runs, she runs, she runs.
Everyone else, so why not me?
But her heart moves the clock hands
Onward, onward relentlessly.

I am a Toothbrush

First I take two fingers
And stuff them in my ears
Another world is taking shape
As this one disappears.

I pretend I am a toothbrush
A scented bar of soap
I'm not the shaking Daddy
Who says his nerves can't cope.

I'm a floating fluffy cloud
I'm an eagle on the wing
I'm a shimmer of the golden sun
The bird who sweetly sings.

I'm a tiny circle
I'm hidden in a square
I'm inside the outside world
Inside I've not a care.

But I think I hear a crash
No, surely I'm mistaken
'Tis the sound inside my head
It cannot be my children.

Why though might I worry?
A rich man, surely, I?
Someone else's job it is
To stop this hue and cry.

For am I not a toothbrush
A scented bar of soap
I'll leave them to the nanny
Surely she can cope.

The Handhold

I caught sight of an old man
In a souped-up invalid car.
Wow! I'd like to have a go
In that, I thought
But then I don't want to
Be crippled and old
I finished first in three races on Sports Day
I'm bright and I'm young and I'm bold.
He looks sad and twisted
And full of pain
He looks like he'd like to
Be young again.
As I worried about the state of his body
Along comes a girl about my age and slowly
Squeezes both his hands, gently does it
And all the age and pain rush out from him
There is electricity in the air
Hope has beaten off despair
I expect to see a young prince
Arise from his invalid car
And show us what he's really like:
Young and able, handsome and smart.
Nothing happens, he sits quite still
But a smile swims across his face –
His granddaughter, her handhold, time and space.

You and Grandma and Me

After the pasta
Out on to the balcony
To view the bright lights
Of this holiday empire
Your face full of dismay
At something so empty.
I thought we could talk
About your Grandma
How she loves you
Looks after you – and me
And as the tears came
Your expression changed
To one of grave concern.
In the light of your eyes
I might, for one split second
Understand life and death
Commune with the continuum.
Back in the lamplight of our room
I felt mundane, all over again.

Our Day out – Parents' View

Righto darling – where to?
The mountains of course
Yes, the children will love
Those long and winding roads
Oh yes <u>and</u> the views
The views – enough to take your breath away
The magnificent mountains, the glittering lakes
The endless blue, blue skies
What a view!
What a surprise!
And when the children
Are overcome and tired
We can stop and admire
Even more of the view
And sip a heavenly cup of tea
From our friendly flask
Whilst the children study the map
And decide on how we might
Continue our journey
To make it our best adventure ever
One with so much to do –
Admiring all those beautiful, beautiful views.

OK, Mum and Dad
We don't need a map.
Just drive as fast as you can
Along the main roads
The straight roads.
It's great to see
The world whizzing by
That way
You don't have to look at anything –
You can concentrate on everything
Else.
See, Mum and Dad
You've taught us
How to sit back and relax –
Think it all through
– And forget about the view.

Transport Poem

My mummy says
She can't think straight
Because I've driven her
Round the bend.
She says I need a crash course
In good behaviour
So that I can learn to stay
On the straight and narrow
Stop living in the fast lane
And never go off the rails.

A Swimming Lesson

In our neighbourhood all the nice
Mums and dads take their darlings swimming.
All the others encourage the art
Of time wasting
And television adoration
And, of course, drowning since
Their children have never been bathing.
In our neighbourhood all the little darlings
Run rings around their dizzy parents
And do some sword fencing
Jazz and tap and ballroom dancing
Whilst their parents sit there gossiping
About the other parents, saying
What a parenting lesson
They could do with learning
And the difference between
Sinking and swimming.

King Cone

Tony's van totters taking corners
The bell tolls Tony's coming
His siren sings of ice ahoy.
Impulsive children are clutching
A sweaty sixpence, tarnished silver
Treasured pennies of bronze faded
Once prisoners in the savings jar
Now free men on the street paraded –
To trade at Tony's gallery
A taste of things to come
Once dormant in the freezer drawer
Now burning at the tongue –
Fab, Mivvi, Split, Screwball
Choc Ice, Rocket, Zoom
- But there is one above the rest
Bow down and give Him room.

Tony asks me – Are you sure you have the money?
This here business is serious
His eyes doubting, asking the question
– You make a purchase so imperious?
Aye Tony, I wouldn't lie Tony,
Mam, she gave me the shilling
And all these coppers here besides
I know the price – and I'm willing.
So Tony takes the silver scoop and smiles
He takes the golden wafer throne
Three bulbous blobs of purest white
– There you are lad, one King Cone.
I pay the ransom, I take the prize
I bow, but I won't look at Tony
For once it's just the King and I –
Set free with stolen money.

Copper in a Vauxhall Viva
Says, "What you doing here?"
"We're only playing football!"
"Well you'd better disappear."

Copper says we're trespassing,
"You'd better clear off home,
This here's for the school you know
Now come on let's be gone."

 "But mister no one's using it."
"That's not the point you see
This here land is Council land
It's where you shouldn't be."

"Oh come on Mister Copper
Why don't you join in?"
"Well maybe just a minute,"
Said the copper with a grin.

His uniform he took it off
We used it for a post
And the copper got excited
When his team scored the most.

So when the siren rang out
He didn't hear at all
They took him off to prison
For scoring an own-goal.

Playing out

It was our Wembley
It was our Wimbledon
It was our Lord's
Our street.

It was gate-post goals
String nets
Cardboard wickets
On our street.

It was late summer nights
Early to rise
Tired legs
On our street.

It was cut and bruise
Sting and graze
No cry-babies
On our street.

It was little kids
Big kids
Inbetweeny kids
On our street.

It was you and me
Him and her
Them and us
On our street.

It was *dare you*
Bet you wouldn't
Run for it!
On our street.

It was big hit
Lost ball
Broken window
On our street.

It was *say sorry*
Shake hands
Start again
On our street.

It was nowhere else
Quite like this
A special place
Our street.

We were the street kids
Our street was our home
Sad to see all the kids have gone
So silent street stands all alone
And rainy tarmac tears flow
Through empty gutters
On and on.

For you, my Love

Oh! If he loved her
The wind would hold her
A flying falcon or albatross
Rising on a thermal
Up there with the sun
And her pillow clouds.
She would wave to him below
And he would blow kisses
Rising even as she
Climbing to meet her.
And so she steels herself
And throws herself from her perch
For a moment her heart beats
Fast as flapping wings
As she manages to hold her head aloft
But her feet are falling
She is leaping
Into his arms.

Love at the Playpark

Lately things have been a little on the
Slide
And I find I can't cope with your mood
Swings
The ups and downs of our
See-saw
Love affair so in a
Roundabout
Way what I'm trying say is
It's time we moved on to a new piece of
Equipment.

The Love Token

Woken
By the shattering
Of cut glass
On polished stone
To find the red rose she gave
Gulping air
Shuddering cold
Drying to death, dismembered
A loss of petal limbs
Traces of carnage litter tiles.
Contemplating my loss
The cat creeps in placing
A friendly paw up on me, whispers
 – It would never have lasted, anyway.

Teaching Forecast (a poem for teachers all at sea)

This is the teaching forecast
Issued at 0800 hours GMT
Today, Wednesday 5th September.
There are warnings of lows
Approaching in all
Areas of the school.
Teachers veering, dizzy.
Storm, cyclonic.
Jordan, Connor, Kylie
Daft becoming moronic.
1200 hours gales unleashing
Playground chaos increasing
– not good.
1400 hours P.E.
Showers. Pupils moderate or good
But becoming variable.
Staff backing into stock room.
Visibility poor, falling (over).
Clearing 1500 hours.
Highs expected.
One or two down the bars.

Lessons to learn

Sometimes
You should let me
Sit still
See, hear and feel
Learn how to be happy
With who I am.

Sometimes
I will work hard
And the concentrate
Of the endeavour
Will suffice
No matter fruits of success.

Presently we will work together
To discover the infinite colour
Shapes and sounds
Of the world around
Us and the one
That lies within.

Feel my hand
It is soft
See my heart
It is open
Listen, my spirit is
Willing, always has been.

In the Mood

What is sad?
What is happy?
It makes me sad
To think I won't be happy again.
I'm so happy
I dread the thought of sadness.
Good things make me happy.
Bad things make me sad.
But is there anything good
About being happy?
Is there anything bad
About being sad?
It makes me happy to know I feel.
I should be sad if I didn't.

Before SATs (exams)

There once was a time
Called the Time before SATs
Then there was topic, English and Maths
And a large nature table
Filled with leaves, seeds
Sticklebacks, tadpoles and honey bees.
Big imaginations abounded
In classrooms filling open minds
Magical stories sounded.
We were taken for walks in woods
Where we studied nothing in particular
We pressed the leaves
Saw them fall and flutter
And felt, that light feeling of life breathing.
Before SATs all the fun in the world
Came into our classroom
And we learnt the two lessons
Childhood and freedom.
And we were never
Examined on them.

Dog and God

God is dog
Spelt backwards
And I do believe
Mine came straight from Heaven
His four paws upon this
Earth serene treading.
His canine smile
Lessens any load,
The angels wove those ears
So soft to the stroke
And wagged the tail on him
That tells me I'm never alone,
Louder than any human can.
Me and him out walking,
I'm not in the real world -
It's a painting
And all the things that are frightening
Are quickly fading
And there's just him and me.
Everything is changing
Into a wilderness
A world of furry kindness
Where dog is God
Spelt backwards.

Sausage Dog

I had a job
Interrogating a sausage dog
I grilled him for hours and hours
Done to a turn
He stared at me and said
You know, you're barking up the wrong tree.

B's

The bee
Is the be all
And end all
For
Without the bee
There wouldn't be
Any fruit at all.

Three Hares

Three hares ran,
Ear and leg
Long and strong
In beauty of being and motion
On a hot crust
Under a lemon sun
He picked them off
With his polished weapon
One by one.

Three men run
And two of them
Are chasing one
Who trips in terror
On the ruined rubble
And is struck dumb
By the double blast
Each one a flash
From a polished gun.

Inside the Orange

Peel the skin
Behold the treasure
Step inside
To take your pleasure

Squeeze the sunshine
Smell the nectar
Bake the earth
Paint the summer

Clear the skies
Take the pollen
Call the bees
And see the orange.

River, Prisoner

From the sweat and spit
Of the sky emerges River.
Clear cold tears crash on
Corrugated earth's core.
River, scared of heights
Runs from the heavens
As frothing rapids or hides
In shadowy holes licking wounds.
His rough tongue scours helpless strata
He squeezes and sinks to new depths
Or else tortured by
His enemy gravity
He rolls on blindly
Cursing the nature of his work
Heaving his tortured form
Onto an unforgiving rock bed.
At night it is the same save
Even the scintillating sun has fled
And an oppressive ink
Of no such succour
Spoils his flashing colour
And at daybreak, in the harsh light
He concludes some were made to suffer.

It rains Flowers

Strange the clouds that float on high
Their colour a deep red
We fear that rain is coming
But flowers fall instead.

A shower of geraniums
Signals break of day
A burst or two of snowdrops
Tumbles from the sky.

A mist of droplet daisies
Beneath our pansy feet
Puddle pelargoniums
Grow upon our streets.

Streams of bright narcissi
Rivulets of gold
Torrents of nasturtium
Down our gutters roll.

Rivers of red roses
Through the valleys roam
Scented petals swimming
Onward to the coast

Where bathing out at sea
Are splendid the surfinia
And the whales and the dolphins
Are lapping up the nectar.

Above the lightning strikes
Close by the thunder boom
Mushroom clouds of poppy seeds
Intensify the gloom.

But soon we see the bluebell sky
Which makes the heavens glow
And helps the brilliant sun to shine
A daffodil yellow.

Orange

Nothing but orange
In the last shreds
Of daylight
Making a marmalade sky.
No blue, no white
Just a dusky cone
To concentrate the eye
And seal the jar
Now that night is nigh.

December Skyline

Someone drew a line in the sky,
Stratus grey above
Clear blue below,
The divide running from church tower to tree top.
Two territories, one dark,
One light.
A marauding mist moves and in a moment
Dense droplets smudge,
Smear a wet finish,
Washing the heavens into one.

The Journeyman

The crackle on the gravel
The rolling of the stone
Footprints on the shifting sand
Where the journeyman must roam

Wishes on the water
Mind up in the mountains
The journeyman his only need
To taste the quenching fountain

Tramps across the countryside
To travel the unknown
He trusts the earth beneath his feet
The journeyman is home

To where his heart is
He who knows much more
Whose eyes are always fixed upon
The ever open door.

Spring Clean

In the garden
The springtime secret's out
The gnomes are humming
The warning alarming:
The Leylandii need trimming
The rockery strimming
The brick needs weaving
The patio bleaching
The pebble dashing
The weeds thrashing
The lawn sterilising
The insects chastising
The sun loungers hosing
The neighbours rehoming
The intruders shooting
All signs of unwanted life removing.

Sight

Hindsight is what
You get
When you have eyes
In the back
Of your head

Highsight is what
You get
When you're eyes are
Too near the top
Of your head

Foresight is what
You get
When you have
Twice as many eyes
In your head

But no sight
Is what you get
When you put two hands
Over the eyes
In your head.

Highlights

My Mummy's had highlights
Put in her hair
Now when Daddy
Misses the football
He can look at
Her instead.

Staff Loss

In the teachers' lost property
This week we have
A memory
A mind
Some marbles
And
It.

Pen Friend

Wanted: Pen friend to share in exciting times

My interests are:
Simply staring or
Sleeping in and watching
TV and paint dry.
Couch potatoes and comas.
Drinking dull dishwater.
Eating ready salted crisps.
Sometimes getting up
And going to the toilet.
Making nothing out of something.
Toe twitching, finger stretching.
Clock watching.
Nail filing, hair growing.
Plain speaking, stamp licking.
Gentle breathing, heart beating,
Distant gazing,
Eye glazing,
Patiently waiting
For your reply.

Look where you're going!

Now listen – I'm not a man
Who goes on and on
And on all about
Nothing

But you mark my words
Let this be a warning -
If you go about not looking
Where you're going
You're going to end up
Bumping into things,
Hundreds of things,
Things full of danger
And then you're going to
End up falling over
And they you'll have to
Go and visit a doctor
And he'll send you to a surgeon
Who'll operate on you
And try to fix you
Good and proper
Like a proper doctor -
But it'll be a new operation
It'll be a bit of experimentation
And they'll be doing examination
And you'll be having in-trepidation
And they'll keep you
In your hospital bed

And one fine day you won't wake up
And you'll be dead
And then you'll meet with God
And he'll ask you
"What have you been doing?"
And you'll feel a bit of a fool –
And look one
But you'll have to tell Him
And He'll say –
Because He's all knowing –
"That's what you get for
Not looking where you're going."

So there you have it
As sure as eggs are eggs
And let that
Be a lesson to you.
Yes, I'm not a man
Who goes on and on and on
About nothing
But you'd better listen to me and God
And, yes, look where you're going.

Telling the Truth

Well yes
In all honesty
As a matter of fact
To tell you the truth
Without a shadow
Of a doubt
Beyond debate
As sure as day
Follows night
Cross my heart and
Hope to die –

I lied.

Capital Loss

Some people say
That in Great Britain
The road that
Leads to rack and ruin
Is strewn
With those
Who missed
The turning
For London.

Don't ask

We're following the leader
The leader the leader
We're following the leader
Wherever he may go!

We're following the leader
The leader the leader –
But why?
I haven't a clue!

Global Warning

When the grey cloud of smog thickens so
That we can hardly breathe
And the green house gases choke and
The earth begins to heat
And there's no escape from the warmth of the sun
And the melt of the glaciers has now begun
So that the sea level rises by and by
And great lakes lie where the land was once dry
And when the low-lying villages are first to go down
Then next it's the fields and the woodlands that drown
And finally Holland is one inland sea
(In the UK we've moved to the mountains and hills)
Then, and only then
I shall swim all the way to London
With a waterproof petition
And ask the Admiral of HMS Houses of Parliament
If he wouldn't mind admitting there's a problem.

Godfather Clock

I saw it all.
Walking down the street
This ancient tall
Time piece.
Left at the market square
And again left
Into the jewellers.
Right!
Everyone against the wall!
It chimed
The Godfather clock
Had struck!
For one second
Time stood still
Hands up
Fingers in the till.

About the Author

David Mason has a Biology degree and has worked in a teaching hospital, for Glaxo Pharmaceuticals and in his own restaurant. His first collection of poetry appeared in 1996 to be followed by over twenty other novels and poetry books for children and adults.

He has taught creative writing and drama in schools since 2000 and has performed poetry to an estimated audience of 200,000 in the intervening years. He runs INSET training sessions on writing poetry.

His wife, Helen, has illustrated many of the books and is the business administrator of their company, Inspire To Write. They have six children.

Please take time to visit the website for more details of his work, books, music and videos at:

www.InspireToWrite.co.uk.